D1392333

WOODBURY

Millennium Cen...

00229850

WITHDRAWN

INTIMATES

INTIMATES

Helen Farish

CAPE POETRY

Published by Jonathan Cape 2005

2 4 6 8 10 9 7 5 3 1

Copyright © Helen Farish 2005

Helen Farish has asserted her right under the Copyright, Designs
and Patents Act 1988 to be identified as the author of this work

This book is sold subject to the condition that it shall not,
by way of trade or otherwise, be lent, resold, hired out, or otherwise
circulated without the publisher's prior consent in any form of binding or
cover other than that in which it is published and without a
similar condition including this condition being imposed
on the subsequent purchaser

First published in Great Britain in 2005 by Jonathan Cape
Random House, 20 Vauxhall Bridge Road, London SW1V 2SA

Random House Australia (Pty) Limited
20 Alfred Street, Milsons Point, Sydney,
New South Wales 2061, Australia

Random House New Zealand Limited
18 Poland Road, Glenfield,
Auckland 10, New Zealand

Random House South Africa (Pty) Limited
Endulini, 5A Jubilee Road, Parktown 2193, South Africa

The Random House Group Limited Reg. No. 954009
www.randomhouse.co.uk

A CIP catalogue record for this book is
available from the British Library

ISBN 0-224-07279-X

Papers used by Random House are natural,
recyclable products made from wood grown in sustainable forests;
the manufacturing processes conform to the environmental
regulations of the country of origin

Typeset by Palimpsest Book Production Limited, Polmont, Stirlingshire

Printed and bound in Great Britain by
Biddles Ltd, King's Lynn, Norfolk

In memory of my father,
Roger Alan Farish

and for my mother,
Mary Anne Farish

Desire, loneliness, the wind in the flowering almond —
surely these are the great, the inexhaustible subjects

Louise Glück

CONTENTS

ACKNOWLEDGEMENTS

Acknowledgements are due to the editors of the following magazines and anthologies:

PN Review, Oxford Magazine, Feminist Review, English Review, Envoi, Tying the Song (Poetry School Anthology, 2000), *Oxford Poets 2004: An Anthology* (Carcanet, 2004), *Being Alive* (Bloodaxe, 2004).

'July' was written in response to and formed part of Christopher Bucklow's exhibition at the Wordsworth Trust, 2004: 'If This Be Not I'.

I should like to thank Keiran Phelan at the Arts Council England, South-East, for a generous bursary. For residencies, I am indebted to the Hawthornden Foundation, the International Centre for Writers and Translators in Rhodes, the Fundación Valparaíso in Spain, and the Wordsworth Trust, Grasmere. My gratitude also to Janet Warren for her generosity.

Finally, thank you to all those who have helped, in various ways, to bring this book about. In particular: Karen Annesen, Christopher Bucklow, Kate Clanchy, Steven Matthews, Bernard O'Donoghue, Robin Robertson, Jo Shapcott, Henry Shukman.

LOOK AT THESE

Seeing you makes me want to lift up my top,
breathe in and say *Look! Look at these!*
I've kept them hidden till now
under loose shirts, Dad's jumpers.

Suddenly I'm offering them
like a woman ready to mate.
I'm holding my breath.
Don't tell me not to.

ALCYONE AND CEYX

It was your leather jacket.
When you left the room I would smell it,
longing to let my hands loose on you,
lust like pub smoke clinging to me.

My father said how could his daughter
love someone with a motorbike,
who drank pints, wore ear-rings?
He warned me what Zeus would do.

I was made a halcyon, you a diver,
our nest wrecked with every tide.
Then out of the blue Zeus stilled the sea
enough for eggs to hatch.

I hate the sky and the water,
the good clean life they smell of.
I long for your leather jacket,
my dress blown tight against me.

AUTO REPLY

As Jesus went on from there, he saw a man named Matthew
sitting at the tax collector's booth. 'Follow me,' he told him,
and Matthew got up and followed him.

On my desk I left a reminder
of what to buy for supper, a scummy
mug of tea, unanswered

emails, no out-of-office
auto reply. I left bank accounts
open, my part-time degree

in piles. I left clothes drying
on the kind of creamy autumnal day
that brings seagulls in from the coast.

I'd fantasised about such a thing thinking
it would take the form of falling
for a woman. I remember how easily

I used to well up – an advert
in which the sea was slowed down
or that movie line: *always be yourself.*

Looking back it's clear
something had risen to the top.
You walked by, skimmed it off.

FEATHERED COYOTE

Like your ancestors who called
prostitutes 'bringers of happiness'
I bring you happiness.

I go to another bed, you follow me,
pull back the sheets, look at me
as though I am a mythical creature,

flowers being made from my hair,
fine grass from my skin.
The *coyote emplumado*

has followed me home from the museum
with an appetite to be the labeller
not the labelled.

Yesterday you called me wife,
amor, chaparrita.
Now my label is the oldest there is

and when you say it in your language
I perform it in mine.
You lie back, feathers everywhere.

WHAT HELD US THERE

They made everyone's heart sing, the folk dancers
with their raggedy band. We were all looking

for an excuse to linger: Saturday morning,
the market, the good feeling wind.

I would have said it was spring, that feeling,
but the summer was well through, almost

looking back on itself. And that was what held us there
though we didn't know it, that we were looking back

on ourselves, the market, the raggedy band,
the singing inside just there and then.

BLINDCRAKE

It was as though the sea
loaded with summer light
was coming in, as though
we had the business of a tide
to attend. This has happened
to me before, realising
in retrospect that the land
in front of me was sea – was why
we were reflective in the way
of people at the sea's edge.
And as with everything
meant to be, it was all
by chance, driving too far
through Redmain, no place
for a U-turn. Blindcrake –
we never intended to visit
but it waited confidently
as though we were ourselves the tide,
the village green an inlet.

BRATHAY

I love to see the symbols on the map –
the cross, the less-than-4-metres-wide road,
the pub (named even). And I love
to see us as symbols and everything
we saw: the two men
chess-playing at Skelwith Fold
in back-porch sunshine, mark it
with T for tranquillity. Put a P
in the graveyard for picnic (teabread,
coffee). An A just there on the verge
for sapling (ash) – how much growth
that summer? And the bend in the road
a double S for smiles (the greengold
light, the veneer of wood-water,
the tilt). And a capital J for summer
(joy), and a D for don't
(let this end), and a G and T left behind
at the pub (empty), and a capital U
for God saying I and the entire
universe wish this walk well.
By the Brathay and the underwater
bubbles that began us, an M
for completion by moonlight.
And all over, write, in full:
The Dazzle of this World.

DOROTHY

Poems on the Naming of Places: IV

We had the time, you see.
And September.
A month in itself like a lake.

And William called it our occupation:
he followed with me
the dandelion seed, the thistle's beard.

Have you ever known that?
The joint untethering of souls,
trusting entirely that the other

will not tug you back?
Shoulders turning in unison,
gradually voices

rising to the surface.
Don't talk to me of marriage. Give me this:
no future tugging me back.

24TH JUNE 1955

Waiting on the doorstep you can hear
the distant intent of the engine
at Hollin Root, now Low Woodside.
Summer sways in its wake.
A farmer's boy in the beck field
looks up too late.

By now you know just how
that red MG will swing in the yard,
how dogs will bark and hens flap,
and how it will feel
to turn in his arms, his hand
on your blue satin waist.

It's easy with the tall-grass wind,
sun bouncing off the bonnet
and destiny's intent
running louder than any engine;
girl, it's easy now to say *I do*
to a lifetime's distance.

IN THE CHURCH OF
ST JOSEPH, PRAGUE

The trams going by outside
were like God. No. 18, No. 22
giving the stone a heart to tremble.

On my knees I knew
no good would come of it,
but when the man behind me sang

with a voice floating inescapably
free of the city, I was staked
to the ground. No. 18, No. 22.

And when the singing died I outwaited
the women in black, knowing by then
trembling would come and go

always. The day had changed.
Until the cleaner came with a key,
I hovered in the doorway watching rain.

NEWLY BORN TWINS

In separate incubators one of the twins was dying.
Against doctor's orders, a nurse put them together.

The strong twin, the one with nothing
pulling her back, she slung
her newly born arm over
the one who was wanting to leave,
and stabilised her heartbeat, made everything
regular in the body of the one who'd already
had enough.

The strong one, she will think
she is God, that she can pull back
life from where it was going.
It will be harder for her
than for the one who already knows
about separation, loneliness, where
they can make you want to go.

TEN TO MIDNIGHT

He pulled away did my Dad, the sailor,
ten to midnight, gently they said,
he pulled away, an experienced hand,
barely a ripple, a magisterial
departure in his whites, my Dad
the sailor, while God's compass
fixed above a hotel bed on a rocky
Italian coastline made me pull away
from my lover crying. Ten to midnight
the crucifix said, ten to midnight.

THE SEA SPEAKS

I think for her,
I take her in.
She doesn't know

that's why she's here.
She thinks she'll find
ways to describe

this matt pewter
my back collects
in the low sun.

I take it all –
disarray, fear.
My intimates.

I've made of them
an existence.
She must learn how.

MOUNT MIRTAGH AND BACK

The emperor Qianlong was obsessed with jade.
To recover the finest boulder from Mount Mirtagh
he sent 1000 men, 100 horses.

Bridges had to be built, mountain paths carved,
in the tender rain roads cut through bluish forests,
and in winter water was frozen for ice-slides.

I want to be like that boulder.
I want bringing me back now to cost you.
I want the irony of how there was a time

I'd have cut the road myself
never to be lost on you,
how there was a time

if my black slip smelt of both of us
I treated it like imperial green jade.
Send me a leaf-shaped agate cup and a thousand

heart-shaped promises. Say you were a fool
to let me slip through your fingers
like water refusing to freeze.

And should the ground ever soften
I'll ask if you remember that first time
you passed me the agate cup saying you would gladly

become a tree, wait all winter to grow a leaf
tender enough to touch my lips.
And in my heart-shaped space then I swore

that for you I'd go to Mount Mirtagh and back
without knowing even where it was
nor how willing you'd be to send me.

RESCUE

She said nothing about how stuck she was,
the foul water, how she'd only approached
in an instinct of thirst, how she was going under
for longer each time. I washed her over and over,

concocted a makeshift pond with good clean water
and a good clean stone, running out
like a child to check on her, a creature
I'd saved whose instinct had led her to filth.

DRIFTS

I've always been able to turn over in bed
to the right or to the left and not feel
my breasts' rearrangement. They are snow,
drifts shaping and reshaping in the night.
It must be thirty years since they settled
on my chest, making themselves
at home. Now I stop myself turning
either way for the pain. I hold them and ask
what the matter is. I apologise for taking
each snowflake for granted. I say I will learn
to live in the world as I used to
when my chest was flat. If it snowed
I couldn't settle until I was out there,
moulding it.

EMPIRE STATE BUILDING

I went straight to the top
to throw us away
in the shape of two cents,
the coins falling
in gloomy parallel lines,
the space between them
void as the no-space
between sky-scrapers feet apart.
But I made the mistake of waiting
till the city lit itself up
in response to dusk
and with dusk
came a wind and with the wind
snow like film-star snow.
Such magic, it was as though
you were by my side
having your say in the proceedings,
making straight lines curvy,
slipping your cold hand
under my coat, finding my bare
back then hanging a right
to my breast, lighting me up.
People left North South and East
to come watch
what was happening on the West side,
and as the 80th floor became the 79th
became the 78th, you said *See,*
we were always worth more than that.

THE RING'S STORY

I was so beautiful I loved it
when he tried to push his finger through me.
He bought a dark chocolate egg
to hide me in. She'd open it.
I'd find myself on her tongue
then her finger, then every night
I'd be there.

I'd always thought of myself as silver,
compared my shine to the heart-stopping sheen
the sun lays on water, an expanse of it,
like a life working out the way you expect.
But it seems I was more hole than metal
and when she took me back I fell in.
Now no one lifts me, slips me on.

THE CHEAPEST FLOWERS

It should just have been a regular
Monday night but you chose it
out of all nights to tell me.

What was special about it?
I really couldn't see, like when you can't see
what someone you love sees

in someone else. It was even cold,
an unregular cold, and it was darker
than regular too and inhospitable,

my regular high street where I know
to find the cheapest flowers, organic bread,
notebooks: what had you done to it?

THE ONES REPLACED

I was his lamby, baba, darling.
It does me good to remember
this will never change. I'll die being

all these names: his surname,
my forenames, the ones replaced
with baba, darling, lamby,

wonderful lass. And the woman
you misread and replaced
sits on the coach thinking *Daddy, Dad*.

JULY

The fifteenth was the day
an ambulance indicated left,
came up the lonning, into the yard.
Swallows made streamers in the air,
oblivious. Hurried out, no time
to look at the garden, his trees –
the merryweather damson, his beth pear,
the keswick apple with the fairy seat,
the czar plums, the old bramleys
with the swing still between.
That was the day following
the last evening he walked up
from the greenhouse, the watering done,
the Solway reddening –
another day gone never to return.
On the sixteenth they upped
the steroids, the high dose prednisode
for the pneumonia overlying
the chronic lung disease. Notes
at the end of his bed said
ten per cent of lungs left.
It was the day the garden
started to grow wild, the day logs stopped
being chopped in the barn. The seventeenth
ten to midnight was the time
nurses came but doctors
couldn't be found and all the days
of his life, 23,535
flocked round, returning to be with him
as if over the years they hadn't gone
never to return, but had flown
to Africa roosting and waiting till all

were needed to accompany him
on this great migration.
Swallows tucked up in the barn were still
between midnight and dawn of the eighteenth.
4 a.m. and they fish the lake the yard makes,
the Solway distantly rolling in, gullies
in the marsh he grew up on the edge of
filling as though there was still
a farmhouse of boys to come running.
And of the 23,000 days
he chose one to hold onto
as percentages fell, oxygen
losing its way to his brain.
The pre-war picnic day, my father
recognisable at seven because
he looks as though he has days
on his mind, focusing not on the camera
but on a spot in the perplexing
distance extending
apparently forever beyond:
days becoming haze.
And up on his knees as though
the moment the shutter closes
he will run, all the days of his life
tucked inside like streamers
one by one to unfurl.

TREASURES

The old coach road on a heat-haze night;
my new jacket; my sudden interest
in swallows; the barn; *Butch Cassidy
and the Sundance Kid*; a cassette recording

of a 17-year-old me; the lost photos;
that Dad hoped in the afterlife
he'd be aware of me; that Dad hoped;
the after life; the advent calendar

John made me; July 28th just gone;
the Ellers' lonning; the monkey clock
at Pickett Howe; our silver Cortina
in the yard; how unremarkable today was.

These are my treasures, and you
wanted only one of them: me
pulling my dress up, poorer
than I've ever been.

SURGERY

That woman who chose to have her breasts removed
rather than live with the fear of cancer
woke up to a flat
bandaged chest,
her body saying *but why*
when I hadn't turned against you?

Like a surgeon
I sever you. Mutilation
or preventative medicine – I'll never know.
But preferable the flat half of the bed
to your hand on my breast one night,
the next on someone else's.

THE ACCIDENT

The disciple of an Indian demigod runs backwards
as a form of prayer.

How can you care enough about anyone,
even a demigod who's had a car accident
to run 500 miles backwards?

I tried it on Rosley road and realised
I wouldn't keep it up,
even if you promised marriage,

said you'd wait 500 miles hence,
fast, and dream about my back.
I'm sorry love.

Not long ago you were a demigod.
I'm trying to pinpoint when
the accident of your humanity occurred.

THE BUTCHER'S BOY

When I went upstairs you were ironing.
When I came down, the board
was taking your weight as you wept.
I couldn't see what had happened.
There was no blood, nothing broken.
It was Remembrance Day radio
and the story of the butcher's boy
that broke your heart in the space between
my going upstairs and coming down.

I don't remember who broke whose
heart, if you stopped loving me
or I you. I don't remember the second
time you wept, how only the floor
could take your weight. I don't remember
broken glass or how such harm
came into our lives. I remember
the butcher's boy – those
who never got to love.

CHINA DOGS

I could think about my mother's sister:
a tea-table to be cleared to the tick
of the monkey clock, jams back

to the pantry, bank up the fire;
outside a bitter Easter and the stretched-out
slowness of life. That's what I could do:

find passageways back to rooms
where afternoons sit quiet as china dogs
and evening comes easy as late snow.

Give me china dogs
to hold onto, I say, let no one
drop me.

LET ME TELL YOU

about the emptinesses,
life punctuated
so rarely by an event:

that until you stop
looking through them,
even what you have

will fall away
like the sound a crow makes,
pure winter.

MESOPLODON PACIFICUS

I have shown myself to you
only as drift and you have presumed
to deduce me from this.

I routinely descend
into abysmal depths,
am far from land, secretive.

But what do you know of my breach,
how the lightless world
bursts off me –

how I can feed on this
for thousands of miles,
the routine weight of air crushing

the sea's surface suddenly
gone, suddenly
an opening into which I pour.

Mesoplodon Pacificus: A species of whale known to exist only because of 'drift'
(stranded specimens). A 'breach' is when the whale clears the surface of the sea
in a spectacular jump.

HERE I AM

dressed, reading,
back together
with the world.
Don't ask me

why we split up
so often,
why it's an on–
off relationship.

I'm only grateful
to be back again,
welcoming myself
to my own chair

over–anxiously,
as with a guest
you sense is inches
from being on her way.

BLINDFOLD

I mustn't be like the woman with nine suitcases
refusing the train south. Two suitcases, no more

on the train. She turned tail, went back
to occupied Hungary, at the border

everything confiscated. I mustn't
be like her. On a night like this. I see myself

on the platform, which seven to give up?
If I could unflinch, be a wheat-haired girl,

or if someone would blindfold me, lead me
like a horse through fire.

FAMILIAR WALK

Except a woman had died by the lakeside.
Thank you, darling wife, for thirty years.
How could a heart

stop beating in such a place?
Or was it the loneliness?
I keep hearing that two

can be as lonely as one.
I don't recollect it, that's all.
I loved you.

THE WHITE GATE

I'm so glad I didn't know
the last time was the last time
we went through the white gate
up the field, that I was able to turn
homeward happy. Lord, protect me

from last times and if you cannot
protect me from last times protect me
from knowing. Take everyone
suddenly, close the gate
suddenly. Tell me nothing.

MANICURE

I'm frightened of dying, I worry
about home, who'll sweep up?
You can only say this

with an unclosed door between us.
What was I doing? Washing my face,
cleaning my nails when I realised

what I'd heard and how I'd failed
to give so many throw-away
if I'm still here's their due.

I bring her into the bathroom,
run hot water, soak her hands then
with the soap she always buys me

lather the scrubbing brush, clean
under her nails, file,
trim and dry them off.

And the thumb that has taken
the brunt of *who'll sweep up*
I smother in Vaseline.

How long is it since I was last
acquainted with these hands? Suddenly
I feel possessive of them, wanting

no undertaker's manicure, the thumb
and forefinger at peace at last:
somebody else sweeping up.

THE OLD KING'S GARDENS

I love you now like I love
unswept paths, unkept groves, like I love
the old hothouse where nothing

will ever grow again, the place an emblem
of pleasure gone by. I couldn't
begin with you all over. What I felt

has acquired the dream-like quality
of those light-thin curtains,
their yearning in the breeze.

THE LIGHTHOUSE OF NAUSET

was removed to a field.
Visitors wonder

does it miss the tides, living on the edge
of emptiness then fullness?

Here there is only the tickle of a cricket,
an out-of-the-way dusk.

The lighthouse says *Listen*.
I thought I had no limits,

could look indefinitely at the longing
light lays on water.

Now I want boundaries:
a hedge, plums, more than enough.

FIFTY YARDS OUT

That couple who saw
the mist-shrouded lake, the boulder,
the dull sword fifty yards out,
and for the next seventeen years

defined their lives by returning,
even regulated their returning
to one weekend in three,
making a science of longing –

don't think it was a waste
of seventeen years.
They are the lucky ones to once
take the right turning on the right day.

PICNIC SPOTS

I love being over you. I can't think
when I've been happier. Being with you
was like the thrill of tightroping

over Niagara. To which compare
life on the other side – a solid bank,
wide grass, picnic spots. Truth is

I barely know who I am now I'm no longer
waiting for you. I only know
one more day would have done it.

PLUM ISLAND

Even as I was parking and looking
at the backs of people on the dune I knew

they'd seen something, the way they
held themselves like the chosen ones.

And I had driven up
late in the day, empty-handed,

as though I could see this anytime:
this acreage of ocean uncrashing, slowed

by the thick coat of day on its back.
Was I half way through life and unprepared

for abundance, for noiseless
waves unscrolling?

AIRING

The day was a hymn,
its ostinato warmth a gift

in which we jobbed about stopping only
after lunch, my dolls

out of their case, sitting on the step
as though the house remembered

and my mother said *you always were
my bonny lass.* Why had we waited

forty years to polish the best
of ourselves, air our finery?

RECORDING

If the house was burning down I'd run
in for it, that plastic box which plays
me back my father, my mother, that car ride: the box
which convinces me it is still going on, the roads
still icy, the night still November and creatures
crouching beyond headlights on the back roads.
It was the 1970s, we hadn't long
had a tape recorder. Dad liked everything
that was new and yearned for everything
that was old and that night he must have known
how old the evening would become. And what I feel
for those two adults and for the girl is how quickly
it will all go, how quickly they will arrive
at the journey's end, how it will come
just like the young girl's sentence snapped off

ODYSSEY

The years I've walked up this path
and back again, *back again*
I've often thought. And now I won't be
back again I promise to be faithful
to the nameless thousand times
I've followed the path to the wood.
Years that run into each other, refuse
to set themselves apart:
I would go so far as to say they were
my great journeys, that when nothing new
drew me along the path, I kept going, not
realising I never came back.

PREY GOD FETICH

Even if I had a prey god fetich
I'd throw it to the ground.
You can go. The dry grass
can have you, the bitter bark
of the purple heart tree.
You'll need a kojaje feather.
On the edge of the mesa
you'll look east. But don't imagine
I'll wait till you become a speck.
I'll turn around before then,
in honour.

BIOPSY

I'm running away with my breasts
to Barcelona, the Canaries.
They've a fancy for some seafront life,
fishermen, local wine.
I'm leaving no more of them at the hospital.
I understand the lump now,
how the cells got together
in a crescent like a young moon,
a smooth-sea boat, a hammock.
All these symbols of longing:
if I had taken notice
they would not have taken shape.

MY FATHER'S DRESSING GOWN

You have no need of it now,
your dressing gown; you are beyond
material possessions, I should release it
with love, let go.

Likewise I am to pray with gratitude
for all unfulfilled desires: *may we be grateful*
for every unfulfilled desire of our hearts.
So your dressing gown is in the bin, amen.

But I released it with pain and kept the cord
hearing you say again, *do you think it's time*
I got another? I've only had this one
since 1955. Thirty-six years of wear

in the bin because I couldn't bear
to keep finding it – first out of your room into mine,
then in the stable, then the barn, each time
more rug-like, each time less you.

In this threadbare mood I think unfulfilled desires
last a lifetime, longing hounded
from room to room till finally
it inhabits all of them.

'GRANT US TIME TO READ
AND PONDER'

The prayer surprises me. Is it permissible
to ask for such things? That afternoon
in the laundry room the light
is a flood river, a workaday annunciation,
a prayer being heard. I stop and ponder
while in the pantry my mother looks for sugar,
picks up first flour, then salt, content
to be making mistakes, to be searching
for what it is permissible to ask.

PROGRAMME

She loves the radio, the freedom it gives
to listen out the back or as she's passing to and fro
or sitting in the half-house half-garden room

on a midsummer's Sunday evening
listening to a three-hour programme on the monsoon,
and the front door is open and the back,

and every now and then the setting light
coming past the lavender she's recently started caring for
and the honeysuckle she never used to notice nor those
    roses

hidden till she chopped back the buddleia – the light
coming past the flowering jasmine and the hanging
    basket
she's so pleased with stops her,

makes her see how much of her life
has been lived in this house,
that she's become who she is here

and what she will remember of these years is not
the times when living alone seemed a problem to solve
but the peace:

looking at a house she has done her best in,
loving small successes, the hanging basket, the picture in
    the half-
house half-garden room, that repotted plant,

and her larger successes – allowing herself the pleasure
of a three-hour programme on the monsoon
sorting through a box of postcards with a green glass of
    gin,

seeing all those places she's been to: but her journey
to this programme, her swept front path, this is
the one she's most proud of.

OUTSIDE THE BAKER'S

for John

She thinks of standing outside the baker's
in no hurry.
It had taken a thousand years to get there.

People she didn't know smiled. Inside
a boy chose a cake, a grandmother
got the right number of loaves.

They came out smiling, the sun
like soft sugar icing making the street
look good enough to eat.

She thinks how for every thousand
there is one like this:
your turn at the head of the queue

being given what you wanted: cakes, bread,
light you hadn't reckoned on like a blessing
you didn't know you needed.

SLATER BRIDGE

Because we sat on the bridge and we'll die

Because the spring after each of our deaths
will lead to a summer of the same
beauty as this

Because in the face of the running water
and the bridge serving centuries
I salute the flag of my love

It is waving there still

COFFIN PATH POEM

My habit of late-light walking
will mirror my life, how in its twilight
I'll rush out saying, how beautiful –
has it been like this all day?